THE LITTLE BOOK OF
Strategic
Negotiation

THE LITTLE BOOKS OF JUSTICE & PEACEBUILDING

Published titles include:

The Little Book of Restorative Justice, by Howard Zehr
The Little Book of Conflict Transformation,
by John Paul Lederach
The Little Book of Family Group Conferences,
New-Zealand Style, by Allan MacRae and Howard Zehr
The Little Book of Strategic Peacebuilding,
by Lisa Schirch
The Little Book of Strategic Negotiation,
by Jayne Seminare Docherty
The Little Book of Circle Processes, by Kay Pranis
The Little Book of Contemplative Photography,
by Howard Zehr

Forthcoming titles or topics include:

The Little Book of Trauma and Peacebuilding
The Little Book of Restorative Discipline for Schools
The Little Book of Biblical Justice
The Little Book of Restorative Justice for Prisoners
The Little Book of Community Dialogue

The Little Books of Justice & Peacebuilding
present, in highly accessible form, key concepts and
practices from the fields of restorative justice, conflict transformation, and peacebuilding. Written by leaders in these
fields, they are designed for practitioners, students, and anyone interested in justice, peace, and conflict resolution.

The Little Books of Justice & Peacebuilding
series is a cooperative effort between the Center for Justice
and Peacebuilding of Eastern Mennonite University
(Howard Zehr, Series General Editor) and publisher Good
Books (Phyllis Pellman Good, Senior Editor).

THE LITTLE BOOK OF
Strategic Negotiation

Negotiating During Turbulent Times

JAYNE SEMINARE DOCHERTY

Good Books

Intercourse, PA 17534
800/762-7171
www.goodbks.com

Cover photograph by Howard Zehr.

Design by Dawn J. Ranck
THE LITTLE BOOK OF STRATEGIC NEGOTIATION
Copyright © 2005 by Good Books, Intercourse, PA 17534
International Standard Book Number: 1-56148-428-8
Library of Congress Catalog Card Number: 2004022059

Library of Congress Cataloging-in-Publication Data

Docherty, Jayne Seminare.
  The little book of strategic negotiation : negotiating during turbulent times /
by Jayne [sic] Seminare Docherty.
       p. cm.
  Includes bibliographical references.
  ISBN 1-56148-428-8 (pbk.)
  1. Negotiation. I. Title.
  BF637.N4D623 2004
  302.3—dc22   2004022059

Table of Contents

Acknowledgments

I owe deep gratitude to the many students I have taught over the years who helped me to refine the ideas in this *Little Book*. They truly were colleagues as well as students.

I am also grateful to Christopher Honeyman and Andrea K. Schneider for inviting me to participate in a November 2003 symposium of scholars and practitioners who teach and practice negotiation. Conversing with a multidisciplinary group about negotiation and then working on the papers we produced for the *Marquette Law Review* helped me to refine my thinking about strategic negotiation.

Thanks also to Howard Zehr for his patience and help while writing this book. Finally, I am deeply indebted to Frank Blechman for generously sharing his knowledge and wisdom about complex, multiparty negotiations.

1.
Negotiating
in
Turbulent Times

Five-year-old Sarah Jones debates with her father about what clothes she will wear to school today. John, her eight-year-old brother, discusses with his mother the appropriate bedtime for a third grader. Their 16-year-old sister, Libby, strikes an agreement with her parents to exchange babysitting services on Saturday morning for gas money and the keys to the car on Saturday night. The parents spend Saturday morning at the car dealership haggling over the purchase of a new car. And, at their Sunday afternoon family meeting, the entire family discusses the relative merits of vacationing at the beach or in the mountains the following summer. This is a family of accomplished negotiators.

Negotiating is the most commonly used form of *conflict resolution*. It involves two or more people (sometimes called "parties") who communicate with one another in order to promote shared understandings, overcome differences, reach compromises, or make mutually beneficial trade-offs. More books, articles, scholarly papers, and dissertations have been written about negotiation than any other method for dealing with human differences. Airport bookstores contain at least one book on negotiation that promises to make you more successful in your business endeavors.

These books tell you when to be a "tough" negotiator and when to be a "soft" negotiator. They promise to reveal the three secrets to "winning" through negotiation, and they give hints about when to share information and when to withhold information during bargaining. Some explain the phases of negotiation; they help you understand that negotiation incorporates agenda-setting, framing the problem, and narrowing the scope of differences between the parties. Most books and manuals on negotiation explore problem-solving, debate, persuasion, bargaining, and a host of other communication activities to achieve agreement around a particular problem. Some of this literature gives detailed explanations of cultural and gender differences in negotiation styles, helps you think about the impact of media attention on a negotiation, or guides you through the complexities of international multiparty negotiations.

> Negotiation involves two or more people or parties who communicate with one another in order to promote shared understandings, overcome differences, reach compromises, or make mutually beneficial trade-offs.

These important and interesting aspects of negotiation are not the subject of this book. Rather, this *Little Book* explores a dimension of negotiation that is not widely understood or even recognized in the literature: how changes in the *context* affect negotiation, and how these might be addressed or incorporated into the negotiation processes.

Changing Contexts

Often, negotiations occur in the context of *established relationships*, as with the Jones family above. Or, they take place within *established social structures* such as the legal system or corporate settings. When negotiators encounter one another within relationships and structures that are generally peaceful and widely accepted as legitimate, they are working within a relatively *stable sense of reality*. Their relationship and interactions are governed by mutually understood norms and rules. These norms and rules are enforced through voluntarily accepted cultural understandings about how things ought to be done, or through formal rules of behavior and contractual obligation, or through some combination of both. This means that in stable settings, the parties can focus on their encounter with one another rather than on managing changes in their surroundings that might affect their relationship.

A stable setting provides mechanisms that support the negotiation process, including the following:

- Mutually accepted rules of behavior.
- Shared norms of fairness.
- Relative certainty that the negotiators have a shared future.
- Institutions (formal or informal) that can enforce negotiated agreements.

We all know, however, that life gets messy. Change happens.

Sometimes change is thrust upon us. Our employer merges with another company or is bought out by a competitor. New government regulations force us to change our ways of doing business. The local school district decides to merge two schools because of a shrinking population.

Sometimes we initiate change. We decide to end our marriage. We participate in an environmental advocacy campaign to force the government to change its regulations and practices. We initiate changes that will lead to greater ethnic, racial, and gender diversity in our workplace. We work in a war-torn country to promote an end to civil strife and violence.

Most books on negotiation almost never ask the hard questions: How do we negotiate when life gets messy? How does an unstable environment alter the process of negotiation? How do we negotiate with one another when the institutions and structures that support negotiation are broken or missing? How do we negotiate with one another when we don't share common understandings about how we should negotiate?

During times of organizational and social change, the mechanisms that support negotiation are unclear, fragile, or completely missing. The parties negotiate in contexts in which there are likely to be:

- Unclear or disputed rules of behavior.
- Competing norms of fairness.
- Uncertainty that they have a shared future.
- Broken, non-existent, or controversial institutions or mechanisms for enforcing negotiated agreements.

Who Can Use This Book?

If you have ever tried to negotiate an issue but had difficulty identifying the parties that need to be at the table, this book is for you. If you have ever reached a negotiated agreement only to have new parties and new issues emerge to upset the agreement, this book is for you. If you have ever wanted to promote social change and were uncertain about how to use negotiation as a strategy for achieving your goals, this book is for you. In other words, this book is for anyone who has encountered a situation where established negotiation practices seemed inadequate.

> This book is an invitation to experiment with new ways of handling difficult negotiations rather than assuming that difficult situations make negotiations impossible.

I have deliberately selected three very different stories about negotiating in turbulent times to illustrate the lessons in this book. One story involves a divorcing couple. Another is about labor negotiations after a corporate merger. The third story deals with a complicated environmental issue. What holds these stories together is the turbulence that surrounds and intrudes upon the negotiation process in each case. This book is not a recipe for negotiation; it is an invitation to creative experimentation. I hope readers will be inspired to experiment with new ways of handling difficult negotiations rather than assuming that difficult situations make negotiations impossible.

Negotiation as a Game?

Books on negotiation explicitly or implicitly treat negotiation as a game or game-like encounter between players. Many of them look only at the tactical elements of the negotiation game. What moves can the party make to maximize her chances of winning?

The game metaphor is helpful if we remember that there are different kinds of games. James P. Carse begins *Finite and Infinite Games* as follows:

> There are two kinds of games. One could be called finite, the other infinite. A finite game is played for the purpose of winning, an infinite game for the purpose of continuing the play.[1]

Negotiation can be played as a finite or an infinite game, or as a finite game played within an infinite game. When negotiators put highest priority on winning a negotiation encounter, even if winning ends their relationship with the other party, they are playing a finite game. When they treat negotiation as one encounter in an ongoing relationship in which they will win some rounds and lose some rounds, they are playing a finite game within the infinite game of their relationship.

In stable settings, negotiators may choose to focus on short-term tactics: What moves will help me win this negotiation? Or they may choose a mix of tactics and strategies that focuses on managing relationships and problems over a longer time frame: How can I maximize my chances of winning this round while keeping the play (relationship) going so that I might win other rounds?

In an unstable setting, negotiators who try to focus only on the tactical level run the risk of losing even if they win. They may ultimately lose if the instability in their context makes implementing their agreement difficult or impossible. Sometimes the changes in their context turn what looks like victory into defeat. In an unstable setting, the negotiators who understand and respond effectively to the conflicts in their turbulent surroundings can negotiate their own problems more effectively and help bring stability to the larger system. To do this, they must think strategically about more than their relationship with the other negotiators at the table. They need to consider the way their negotiation game is embedded in, influenced by, and capable of altering the infinite game of the social relationships that make up the context in which they live and work.

Why I Have Written This Book

In my work, I find myself in the company of two different groups of people concerned with issues of conflict resolution or transformation. One group, negotiation scholars and professional negotiators, is inclined to think of negotiation as a finite game, even if that game is set inside an infinite game of human relationships. Many of them describe negotiation as if it always occurs in stable settings, with clear rules and boundaries and obvious winners and losers.

The other group, peace activists and peace-builders, is inclined to view negotiation with deep suspicion. Many of them see the world as an uneven playing field on which powerful parties oppress weaker parties. Since weaker parties will inevitably lose the finite game of negotiation, it is better not to play the game at all. Peace will be created by focusing energy on changing the playing field and the rules of play, not by negotiating specific issues or problems with powerful oppressors.

I believe both groups are wrong. Those who treat negotiation as a finite game in a stable context minimize the full complexity of the conflicts that brought the parties to the negotiation table. They may negotiate agreements that put a bandage on deep-rooted and intractable conflicts, thereby creating greater social turmoil. The peace they win in these situations is fleeting at best. Those who think negotiation is always "selling out" to the powerful parties focus on the sources of deep-rooted conflicts, but they overlook the option of negotiating strategically to transform conflict and change unjust social systems. Both groups would benefit from thinking about how to negotiate strategically in unstable settings.

Negotiating strategically in an unstable context involves:

- Focusing on the immediate problems *and* the long-term relationships between the parties.
- Managing the turmoil in the context *and* the interactions at the negotiation table.
- Working to bolster or create and sustain the social structure and/or the political will that supports the negotiation process and the agreement reached by the negotiators.

Thinking About the Big Picture

To successfully negotiate problems in the absence of structures that organize and support the negotiation, negotiators must also manage activities that are normally handled in a quiet, routine manner by established institutions. Consequently, they must depend on the goodwill and the support of other parties not at the table to implement and sustain their agreement. No matter how good, fair, creative, and just an agreement is, others will not support it if the negotiators do not consult with and educate them about the agreement. That education and consultation need to start before formal negotiations convene and need to continue after an agreement is reached.

We can think of strategic negotiation as a layered set of interactions that include primary negotiations at the table and shadow negotiations with parties who are not at the table. (See Figure 1 on page 14.) The primary negotiations occur at the core. In the next layer out, we find shadow negotiations with parties that have a stake in the conflict but who have decided not to negotiate. Included in the stakeholder group are institutions and organizations that may have an interest in the conflict. In the case of a family conflict, such institutions may include the extended family or religious community. In workplace conflicts, unions may occupy this role. Or in public conflicts, large bureaucracies or nongovernmental organizations may fall into this category.

> Strategic negotiation is a layered set of interactions that include primary and shadow negotiations.

These institutions and organizations are often key players when it comes to implementing an agreement, but negotiators representing these parties are frequently able to speak only for one small portion of the organization. Consequently, the internal negotiations within those organizations are extremely important when it comes time to implement and sustain an agreement.

Surrounding the organized stakeholder groups is the general public of unorganized individuals who can be mobilized to either support or challenge a negotiated agreement. If negotiators pay attention to the needs of the general public and plan ahead to present their agreement to

Figure 1
Negotiating Strategically Includes
Primary Negotiators and Shadow Negotiators

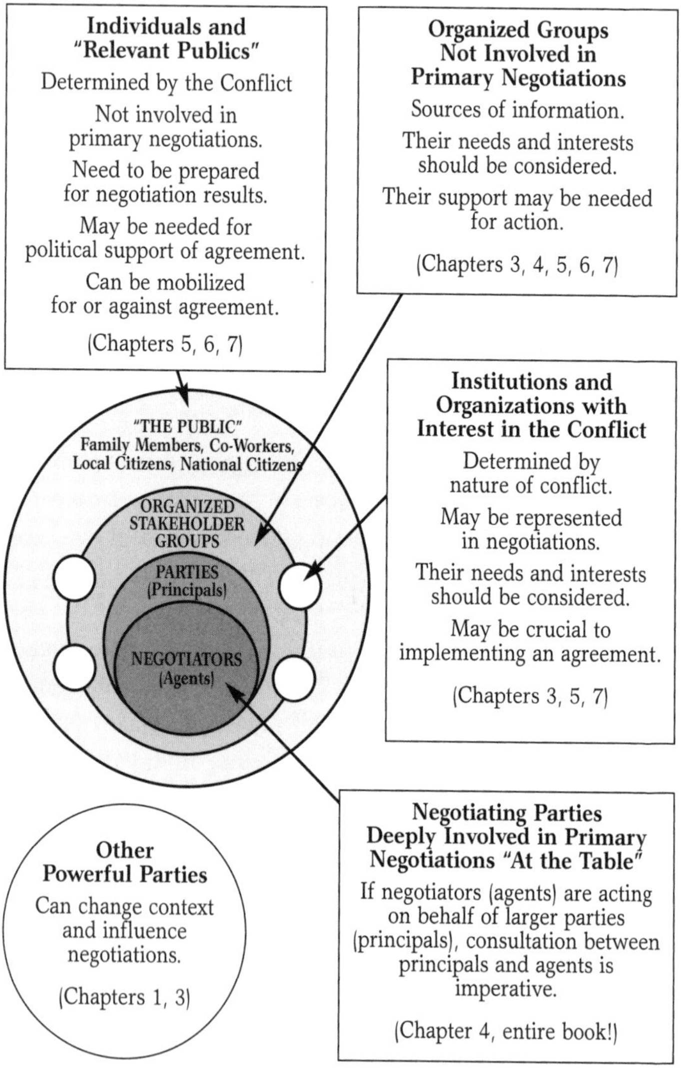

Individuals and "Relevant Publics"

Determined by the Conflict

Not involved in primary negotiations.

Need to be prepared for negotiation results.

May be needed for political support of agreement.

Can be mobilized for or against agreement.

(Chapters 5, 6, 7)

Organized Groups Not Involved in Primary Negotiations

Sources of information.

Their needs and interests should be considered.

Their support may be needed for action.

(Chapters 3, 4, 5, 6, 7)

"THE PUBLIC"
Family Members, Co-Workers, Local Citizens, National Citizens

ORGANIZED STAKEHOLDER GROUPS

PARTIES (Principals)

NEGOTIATORS (Agents)

Institutions and Organizations with Interest in the Conflict

Determined by nature of conflict.

May be represented in negotiations.

Their needs and interests should be considered.

May be crucial to implementing an agreement.

(Chapters 3, 5, 7)

Other Powerful Parties

Can change context and influence negotiations.

(Chapters 1, 3)

Negotiating Parties Deeply Involved in Primary Negotiations "At the Table"

If negotiators (agents) are acting on behalf of larger parties (principals), consultation between principals and agents is imperative.

(Chapter 4, entire book!)

the public, they can minimize the chances that groups will form to oppose the results of their negotiation.

Finally, in the most unstable and difficult contexts, powerful parties not directly involved in the conflict or in the problem being negotiated may take actions that alter the context or bring significant pressure to bear on the negotiators, often for reasons only tangentially related to the central conflict. An example of this is the War on Terrorism after September 11, 2001. The United States labeled a number of groups that were involved in negotiations to end civil conflicts around the world as terrorist organizations. In some cases, the United States began funneling additional military and financial resources to the governments negotiating with these groups, which essentially halted the negotiations.

Clearly, negotiators cannot predict events like September 11, and they cannot do much to control the reactions of powerful parties such as the United States. However, in many cases, it is possible to influence the actions of powerful external parties, such as Congress or the media, if negotiating parties take a united position in relation to those powerful actors. In this book, I will address the cases where the parties can exert influence on powerful actors outside the negotiation, but I do want to acknowledge that there are some cases where influencing powerful external actors is all but impossible.

Three Stories

Throughout this book, we will return to three stories which illustrate negotiation during times of change.[2] In each chapter, these stories will be used to illustrate the points and suggest ways to help situations in which you are an observer or are involved.

Jean and Sam End Their Marriage

Jean and Sam have been married for 24 years. They have a 16-year-old daughter named Jennifer. They have decided to divorce, and they want to negotiate the terms of their divorce agreement themselves rather than use attorneys to litigate their divorce.

Jean and Sam need to determine how to allocate assets and debt; who is responsible to provide for Jennifer's needs, including her education; how they will continue to make parenting decisions together; how to share visitation rights; where Jennifer will spend holidays; and how they will provide for continued health insurance for Jean.

The Hard Work of a Corporate Merger

Representatives from the union and the management of Acme-Zocon Corporation meet to renegotiate the labor contract that governs 30 percent of the employees in the company. This is the first such negotiation since Acme Company and Zocon Corporation merged.

Since the merger, there have been two management reorganizations and a 25 percent downsizing in two major divisions of the company. Negotiations will include the usual wage and benefit issues for union employees, plus the question of which disciplinary appeals process will be used for union employees—the one negotiated with Acme or the one negotiated with Zocon prior to the merger.

Making Ecosystem Management a Reality

Employees of two federal agencies meet with ranchers and representatives of environmental advocacy groups to discuss how they will determine the number of cattle to graze on federal lands. The relationships among these parties have been conflicted and litigious. Environmental groups have sued the agencies to block them from issuing grazing permits. Some environmental groups want all cattle removed from public lands; other groups think some grazing is acceptable, but they want to modify the processes for determining how many cattle can be grazed. Some ranchers are in favor of changing ranching practices, while others have resisted these changes. Some ranchers distinguish between locally-based environmental groups and national environmental groups, giving the former credibility and legitimacy and describing the latter as outsiders interfering in things they don't understand.

New federal mandates require that the decisions on grazing be made using "ecosystem management strategies," but no one is really clear what ecosystem management looks like. Furthermore, the agencies do not have standard operating procedures in place for managing at an ecosystem level.

2.
Negotiation Occurs in a Negotiated Context

Negotiation involves parties who have a conflict or dispute in a process to find a nonviolent solution to their problem. Negotiation may be done competitively: each party tries to maximize her own gains and minimize her own losses. Or negotiation may be done cooperatively: the parties try to figure out how each party can get the most satisfactory solution to its problem. In most cases, parties move between competitive and cooperative approaches depending on the issue and the nature of their relationship and a host of other factors.

A hallmark of much negotiation literature is the idea that negotiators present their *positions* (their stated objectives or goals), but that they are really more motivated by their *interests* (what they really want) and their *needs* (what they actually need in order to survive). The classic example of positions versus interests is the case of two girls arguing over who will get the last orange in the house. Each insists on having the whole orange, and both claim that splitting the orange in half (distributive bargaining) is not an option. Their mother asks each girl why she needs the orange. One girl wants the fruit and juice for a recipe, while the other girl wants the peel for a different recipe. The win-win (integrative bargaining) solution is that one girl gets all the peel while the other gets all the fruit and juice.

Unfortunately, life is usually a lot more complicated than this case. Not only is it difficult to find a win-win or integrative outcome in negotiation, in many cases there are large conflicts over who belongs at the negotiation table, what the real issues are to be negotiated, and how negotiations should be structured or managed.

Minimal Requirements for Negotiation

In order to negotiate, the parties must first agree that they have a conflict or dispute, *and* they must also agree that negotiation is an appropriate process for handling their situation. In the Jones family, five-year-old Sarah is permitted to negotiate what she will wear to school. By contrast, the Harrison parents do not recognize their son, Bobby, Sarah's playmate, as an acceptable negotiation partner, at least not on this issue. If Bobby wants to negotiate his choice of apparel, he will first need to renegotiate his family's unspoken rules of parent/child roles. Bobby instinctively understands this when he wails, "*Sarah* gets to pick *her* clothes!"

Bobby's mother, frustrated with her family's daily battle over dressing for school, talks with Sarah's mother, who explains what things are negotiable and not negotiable in her family. The next day, Bobby and his mother decide together what he will wear to school. In this case,

Bobby's mother altered her sense of reality in order to accept Bobby as a negotiating partner and his choice of clothes as a negotiable issue. In fact, Bobby's mother altered something that many people think of as difficult to change—her sense of identity as a mother and her internal story about what is expected of a "good mother."

This simple story illustrates that all negotiations over a particular issue or problem occur within a context that is, itself, negotiated and subject to change. During any negotiation, the parties can and usually do move from negotiating a particular problem to negotiating the context in which they operate. We can hold this important feature of negotiation in mind using the model in Figure 2.[3]

Figure 2
Parties Can Move Back and Forth Between Two Types of Negotiation

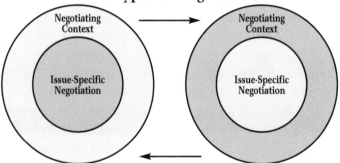

When the context is stable and validated by all parties, they can focus primarily on issue-specific negotiation.

When the context is in turmoil, under question, or being renegotiated, they must focus more energy on negotiating the context.

For parties to negotiate an issue, their context *must* include the following features:

- The parties must have a mutually acknowledged relationship.

- The parties must agree that there is a conflict or dispute.
- They must also agree that the conflict or dispute is amenable to negotiation.
- Finally, each party must recognize the other as a legitimate negotiation partner.

In an unstable context, the four conditions necessary for negotiation may be fragile or tenuous. Therefore, energy must be directed toward building up the necessary conditions for negotiating issues or problems.

To a lesser extent, parties involved in a negotiation also need to have some sense of a shared world. It is not absolutely necessary that the parties fully share a single understanding of reality, but we can say negotiation is easier if:

> Negotiations over a particular issue or problem occur within a context that is, itself, negotiated and subject to change.

- The parties agree about those parts of their context that are most relevant to the primary issue in their negotiations.
- The parties share tacit rules, norms, and expectations about how the negotiation will proceed.
- The parties recognize the legitimacy of the same potential arbiters ("referees" or "judges") if they reach an impasse in their negotiation.

These ideal conditions are less likely to hold true during times of change. In such cases, energy and attention must be divided between negotiating the context and negotiating particular issues. This divided attention is the key feature that distinguishes negotiating during times of change from negotiating in a relatively stable setting.

Practical Implications

Whenever we try to negotiate, there may be problems meeting the necessary conditions for negotiation. Perhaps some parties see a conflict while others are unaware of a problem. This is particularly likely in cases of great power disparity or when the parties relate to one another only indirectly. For example, rank-and-file workers at Acme-Zocon probably see problems resulting from the merger that top management doesn't recognize. In a more extreme form of this problem, some parties may deny the very existence of other parties in the conflict. Or, they may recognize their existence but deny their right to be involved in negotiations.

Sometimes parties must use confrontational tactics to create the conditions for negotiation. However, confrontation should be used carefully in order to avoid locking the parties into a sense of good (self) and evil (other) that prevents moving to the negotiation table. Violent or aggressive confrontational tactics can leave residues of anger and pain that impede the ability to work cooperatively with others in negotiation. But confrontation used well and carefully can create the necessary conditions for negotiation.[4]

3.
Changes in Context Can Create Turbulence in Negotiations

Parties sometimes use confrontational tactics to "force" another party to negotiate or to define the issues. To use such tactics effectively, we need to understand the instability that makes it difficult for parties to recognize each other as negotiation partners and to reach agreement about negotiable issues. The three cases from Chapter 1 illustrate a variety of ways that such turmoil in the surrounding environment can make negotiation more difficult.

Jean and Sam End Their Marriage

Jean and Sam must negotiate some difficult issues: allocating assets and debt, providing for Jennifer's needs, determining how they will continue to make parenting decisions together, agreeing to visitation rights, determining where Jennifer will spend holidays, and agreeing

---

how they will provide for continued health insurance for Jean. But just as important as sorting out these issues, Jean and Sam are reconfiguring their worlds to include the reality that they will continue to be co-parents though no longer husband and wife.

Renegotiating the reality of their relationship will be profoundly unsettling to Jean and Sam even if they both want the divorce. Reality is not negotiated rationally; we do not bargain or trade our sense of our lives as a coherent whole. Rather, we each tell stories of our lives, autobiographical accounts that give our lives meaning and shape our sense of identity. Jean and Sam must each retell and reshape the stories of their relationship and their identities as part of moving from being marriage partners to being the divorced parents of Jennifer.

How do Jean and Sam fare on the checklist of requirements for negotiation?

- They agree that they have a conflict or dispute.
- They agree that negotiation is the best way to deal with their conflict.
- They recognize each other as legitimate negotiating partners.
- They have agreed to a preliminary list of issues they need to address.
- They have a mutually acknowledged relationship, *but it is a relationship that is in transition as they reshape the story of their marriage and work toward a shared vision of their future relationship.*

This last factor points to the instability in Jean and Sam's context. The complexity of an unstable situation will affect their negotiation because the changing nature of that relationship is precisely what has brought Jean and Sam to the negotiation table. Different understandings of their future relationship as co-parents and the emotionally difficult process of unhooking their identities from their marriage create instability in their mutually acknowledged relationship. The instability in their relationship is most likely to manifest itself in disagreements over some combination of the following four areas:

- Issue identification: What is being negotiated or what is negotiable?
- What norms of behavior will govern the process of negotiation?
- What standards of fairness will be used to help resolve disagreements over issues?
- What outside parties will be used to help resolve any impasse in the negotiation?

If Jean and Sam do not understand the difficult process of renegotiating their identities and retelling their stories, when they get stuck in their negotiations they are likely to accuse each other of being unreasonable, inaccurate, or overly emotional. If, on the other hand, they are able to retell the stories of their lives in ways that allow both of them to move forward with their lives, the negotiations will yield more satisfactory and enduring agreements.

The case of Jean and Sam points to an important feature of the *context* within which negotiations occur: our shared social realities are products of our meaning-making, and *stories* are a central part of the way we give meaning to our world. The types of activities most often associated with negotiation are bargaining, problem-solving, debate, and persuasion. To engage in these activities, parties use *instrumental language* and *relational language.* Instrumental language is rational and analytical; it is the language of logic and bargaining. Relational language is the language we use to express connection or disconnection with others. Negotiators use these two forms of language together to create and sustain a relationship in which they can solve problems and resolve disputes.

In contrast, the activities we use to negotiate our shared reality—or the context in which we are negotiating—involve naming the world (what is out there and what does it mean?) and naming ourselves and others (who am I and who are you?). The types of language we use to negotiate our shared reality are *storytelling, metaphors, and references to powerful images or symbols.* These forms of language are richer and more complex than the language of issue negotiation; they are associated with the human capacity for giving meaning to the world, indeed the human capacity to *create* a social world of relationships and institutions.

> Changing contexts require shared realities and meanings to be negotiated. This involves *stories, metaphors,* and *symbols.*

In order to reach agreements about the specific issues they are addressing in their divorce, Jean and Sam must also take the time to tell stories about who they are and who they will be in relation to one another. Storytelling also opens the space for grieving, which is an important part of any negotiation process in which the parties are coping with a changing context that involves loss.

The Hard Work of a Corporate Merger

When representatives from labor and management at the newly merged Acme-Zocon Corporation sit down to negotiate a new labor contract for 30 percent of the company's workforce, they are operating within the highly formalized and institutionalized set of practices that govern labor negotiations.

- They recognize their relationship.
- They accept that negotiation is the proper way to handle their differences.
- They acknowledge each other as legitimate negotiators.
- They probably share some unspoken rules and norms about how to negotiate.
- The parties probably agree to the same potential arbiters ("referees" or "judges") if they reach an impasse in their negotiation.

In this situation, the parties' confidence in their ability to handle this "routine" negotiation is likely to lead to problems, because their surroundings have changed more than they realize.

Every company develops a corporate culture—shared norms, values, and expectations about proper behavior. Merging corporate cultures is neither easy nor conflict-free, and the problems are exacerbated by the fact that this soft side of a merger is rarely given adequate attention during the merger negotiations. Old "we" and "they" identities die hard and are likely to persist for some time. Furthermore, mergers are rarely a marriage of equals, and they are sometimes the result of hostile takeovers. When a merger is followed by reorganization and downsizing, employees watch closely to see which employees benefit and which employees suffer from the merger.

As they start their negotiations, the parties are likely to assume they share tacit rules, norms, and expectations about how the negotiation will proceed, and to some extent they do. However, every corporation plays out the script of labor negotiations according to its own unspoken cultural norms, and the Acme-Zocon negotiators may be surprised at how much their norms vary. The issues of corporate culture are most likely to emerge openly during the negotiations over which disciplinary appeals process will govern relationships in the merged company, but these issues will be at play in other discussions as well.

On the surface, the Acme-Zocon negotiators may appear to agree about those parts of their negotiated reality that are most relevant to their issue negotiations. But subsurface negotiations about which culture (Acme or Zocon) will dominate, or how they will merge their cultures, will require careful attention, too. Unfortunately, these are not the types of issues that most labor negotiators readily acknowledge or accommodate.

A further difficulty for Acme-Zocon negotiators arises out of the fact that the changes created by the corporate merger are probably unevenly validated in the organization. If we think of the organization as a pyramid, with top leadership, middle management, and the workers, the merger was negotiated at the top levels, possibly (but not definitely) with consultation at the middle management level, and with little or no consultation of the workers. Yet, middle management and the workers must renegotiate their relationships across the Acme-Zocon cultural divide in order for the company to function effectively. Figure 3 on page 29 illustrates the need to pay attention to the ways that changes in context affect members of an organization or community differently.[5]

From the Acme-Zocon case we learn that change is not always equally welcomed by all of the parties in a con-

Figure 3
Change is Not Experienced Uniformly
by All Actors in a System

Types of Actors	Involvement in Merger	
Level 1: Top leadership, CEO, and Vice Presidents and their advisors.	Negotiated the merger, made the decisions, and have an interest in seeing that it succeeds.	**FEW** ↑
	Don't have significant direct responsibility for the renegotiation of daily procedures.	
Level 2: Middle management, heads of various divisions, and their assistants	Were minimally consulted in the merger negotiations, if they were consulted at all, but they have the responsibility for making the merger work.	Affected Population
	Need to lead the negotiation of all of the daily details of the merger.	
	May have mixed feelings about the merger.	
Level 3: Workers	Were not consulted about the merger but feel the effects daily in their workplace.	
	Need to accommodate the changes by renegotiating daily routines and norms and procedures.	
	May not see the merger as positive if it has been associated with job losses and/or wage and benefit reductions.	**MANY** ↓

flict, and this creates turbulence for negotiators. Some employees may be ready to move ahead and embrace a future-oriented story of a shared Acme-Zocon identity. Other employees may need to grieve the loss of identity as well as the loss of jobs that came with the merger. Trying to move directly into problem-solving and bargaining when the parties have different feelings about the changes in their relationship is likely to evoke resistance to the negotiated agreement.

Making Ecosystem Management a Reality

If the cases of Jean and Sam and Acme-Zocon seem challenging, they are nothing compared to the negotiations over implementing ecosystem management strategies on federally-owned lands. In this case, we have:

- Parties that are internally divided. Not all ranchers take the same approach to the conflict, not all environmentalists take the same approach to the conflict, and the federal agencies are beset by internal divisions and competition among the agencies.

- Loosely organized parties that are difficult to identify. Which organized environmental groups will be included in negotiations? What do you do about ranchers who don't want to participate in the process?

- Representatives from large bureaucracies who cannot speak for their entire organization, but whose ability to bring resources to bear on the problem may ultimately determine the success of a negotiated outcome.

- Parties that must, by their nature, negotiate through representatives, but whose representatives are likely to be plagued by conflicts within their parties.

- A set of issues so large and complex that framing the negotiation to a manageable agenda will be difficult.
- Actors (particularly Congress and the political appointees in the federal agencies) who are not at the negotiation table, but who have the power to make changes in the context that demand immediate attention from the parties.

In this setting, pre-negotiation is as important as what happens at the negotiation table. Negotiating to negotiate includes framing the issues, selecting the particular locale and the problem on which to focus negotiations, establishing relationships among the parties adequate to support negotiation, and setting a time frame for negotiations. Negotiating to negotiate frequently involves using other conflict resolution or conflict transformation processes, including but not limited to dialogues, discussion groups, and visioning processes to improve relationships and develop a shared understanding of problems before negotiations commence.

> When a context is extremely unstable, sometimes the parties must give as much attention to "negotiating to negotiate" as they give to the negotiation itself.

Let's assume, then, that the parties have refined the original problem in the following ways. Representatives from environmental groups and ranchers who have been participating in other dialogue processes for several years agree with the local managers of two federal agencies in a specific area of New Mexico that they are ready to negotiate four issues. These issues are: what information (scientific/research data) about the ecosystem is needed to make decisions about ecosystem health prior to allocating grazing permits in the area, who will collect the data, how the data will be analyzed, and by whom. The negotiation will focus on planning for one small area for the next five to 10 years. The participants recognize that this is an experimental endeavor—a new approach to cooperative planning—and that this negotiation will not resolve the wider social and political conflict over grazing rights on federal lands. However, this limited experiment might demonstrate a model for negotiating ecosystem management practices that can be replicated elsewhere in the federal lands system.

Having agreed to negotiate, we can now say that:

- The participants in this process do recognize their relationship with one another, but at least two parties (environmentalists and ranchers) are also tied to other organizations that view this level of cooperation with suspicion.

- These parties accept that negotiation is the proper way to handle their differences over the very limited issues and problems they have identified, but they do not, therefore, assume that negotiation is the only way they will manage their conflicts. They might at other times or for other causes resort to litigation or other less cooperative activities.

- They acknowledge each other as legitimate negotiators for these issues, but much about the issues remains unclear.

- They will need to develop norms and expectations about negotiation since this is a new process for them.

- The parties probably do not recognize the legitimacy of the same potential arbiters ("referees" or "judges") if they reach an impasse in their negotiation. Therefore, failure in negotiation is likely to result in resumed hostility and confrontational tactics.

We can readily see that relationships are fragile and the issues to be negotiated are complex.

Turbulence will also manifest itself in the negotiations when others who are not party to the conversation act in ways that alter the context in which the negotiators are operating. So, if Congress passes new legislation—quite possibly at the behest of environmentalist or ranching advocacy groups not participating in the negotiation—how will this affect the issues on the table and the relationships among the negotiators? Or, if another environmental group sues the land-management agencies during the negotiation process, how will the parties respond? Or, if a cattleman's organization begins a public advocacy campaign on behalf of ranchers, how will the parties respond? Or, if a new director of one of the agencies re-organizes staff and reprioritizes agency goals, how will the agency representatives be affected?

> Turbulence will occur when others who are not party to the conversation act in ways that alter the context of the negotiations.

Figure 4 illustrates the complexity of the "behind-the-table-negotiations" that are likely to affect the primary negotiations. It also includes parties with the power to take actions that will affect the negotiation.

This negotiation potentially threatens the participants' identities. Environmentalists who have been suing to prevent grazing on federal lands must retell the story of

Figure 4
Negotiators Need to Manage Main-Table and Behind-the-Table Negotiations

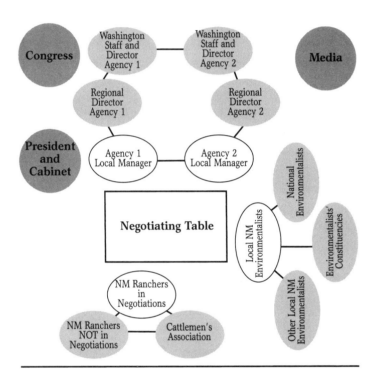

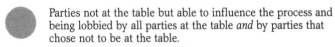

Parties not at the table but able to influence the process and being lobbied by all parties at the table *and* by parties that chose not to be at the table.

Parties not at the table but potentially able to influence the parties at the table and/or punish them for being at the table.

Parties at the table; they must negotiate with and may be influenced by parties not at the table.

Lines of communication between parties at the table and those not at the table. May be cooperative or hostile.

their own identity and the identity of the ranchers in order to participate in this negotiation. Likewise, ranchers must think seriously about how they will change their practices and self-identity to incorporate ecosystem health issues. Can a rancher uphold traditional cowboy values and identity while working with environmentalist advocacy groups that seem to devalue ranching as a way of life? The identity threats are further exacerbated because both environmentalists and ranchers need to distance themselves from others in their respective "camps" in order to negotiate with one another.

The turbulence from the context will appear whenever the parties negotiate sensitive issues. For example, at some point they will need to decide whether the socioeconomic health of local communities should be measured, or whether ecosystem health is only about the natural environment. They will also need to decide whether ranchers and environmentalists will be actively involved in data collection and monitoring systems, or whether those functions will remain in the hands of government scientists. A concession on these issues further separates the negotiators from other groups with whom they have identified themselves, making these issues even more complicated than one might anticipate.

Obviously, there are many ways that this negotiation might be driven off track by external factors. To succeed in their negotiations, the parties at the table will also need to manage negotiations with other parties successfully.

Practical Implications

In stable contexts, established forums or arenas for negotiation help define the parties and the issues. In a legal setting, the legal system defines the plaintiff, the defendant, and legitimate issues for negotiation. In a business setting, we may negotiate a contract that is shaped largely by the norms and expectations of commercial interactions. Our case studies illustrate three different forum problems:

- The forum is clear, stable, and acceptable to all of the parties, but turbulence in their relationship requires that they use the forum carefully if they want to address all of their issues (Jean and Sam's divorce).
- The forum appears clear and stable but is more fragile than the parties think and perhaps too narrow to address all of the issues (Acme-Zocon merger).
- The unstable context provides parties with a large array of forums for advancing their cause (courts, lobbying Congress, mobilizing public opinion) but no forum for *negotiating* that can include all of the parties and issues (ecosystem management case).

The parties can make better decisions about whether they have a forum problem if they begin with an assessment of the conflict in its entirety.[6]

If it is clear that the relevant parties are at the table, they can ask what issues are not being addressed in their negotiations and why not. It is not adequate to blame the forum for failing to accommodate the missing issues, since any established arena for negotiation carries norms and expectations about the types of issues being negotiated. If this is the problem, the parties can figure out ways to stretch the forum to accommodate the missing issues.

If there is some doubt that all the parties are at the table, they can use Figure 1 (page 14) and Figure 4 (page 34) to identify other parties with a stake in the conflict. Then they can figure out who is not able to enter the negotiation forum as it is currently configured and why. In many cases, it is impossible to create a forum that can accommodate all of the parties involved in the conflict. Some parties may choose not to negotiate. Others may prefer to participate only indirectly in the behind-the-table shadow negotiations. But if the negotiators have a clear, shared understanding of the larger conflict, they can create the most inclusive negotiating forum possible. They can also work more effectively with parties not at the table to ensure that the agreements they negotiate are acceptable to others and, therefore, more likely to be implemented.

4.
Preparing to Negotiate Strategically

Negotiation is never the only option for addressing conflicts. Therefore, parties considering negotiation need to ask:

- Is negotiation the best option for addressing our issues and problems?
- What are the alternatives to negotiation?

Parties should assess their Best Alternative to a Negotiated Agreement (BATNA) both before entering into negotiations and repeatedly during negotiation, since they usually have the option to leave negotiation and enter into other processes for addressing their conflict.

In turbulent times, the parties may not have clear BATNAs.

Parties working in the context of instability or change may find it difficult to assess their BATNA. Alternative conflict resolution options may be unclear. The process of negotiation itself may appear risky and fragile because it lacks solid institutional support. In such cases, the parties may need to create relationships and systems that will support the negotiation process. Furthermore, negotiation may only be useful for addressing one small portion of the larger conflict, so that negotiation may need to be coordinated with other conflict resolution activities before, during, and after the negotiators do their work.

If the parties decide to negotiate, they need to be clear about the scope and limitations of negotiation in a context of change and instability. They need to identify:

- What problems or issues they will negotiate.
- What problems or issues they will address using other means.
- What other groups or parties need to be prepared for the negotiation process and for the outcomes of negotiation.
- How this negotiation fits into other processes for managing specific problems or issues, their larger relationship, and the changing context.

Jean and Sam End Their Marriage

Divorce is a legal process shaped by the state through the courts. In this respect, Jean and Sam are working in a stable context that offers them the choice between litigation and negotiation. The instability in their situation arises not out of any fragility in the system regulating their negotiation, but out of their need to renegotiate their personal relationships and identities while they are working through the legal issues of their divorce. Assuming they decide to try negotiation, Jean and Sam first need to make some important strategic decisions.

Do they want to negotiate face-to-face or through their attorneys? Negotiating face-to-face allows space to address the problem of redefining their personal relationship, thereby increasing their control over the central source of turbulence in their lives. Face-to-face negotiation minimizes the risk of miscommunication. It can also prevent the problem of an attorney focusing only on the legal issues of rights and responsibilities without taking into account the personal issues of relationship. On the other hand, divorcing couples who negotiate face-to-face are forced to juggle rational problem-solving and highly emotional encounters at the same time. This is why Jean and Sam need to decide whether to use a mediator to help them with the process of negotiation.

Changing contexts make it difficult to assess conflict resolution options.

If they use a mediator, they need to decide what kind of mediator to employ: an attorney, a counselor, or a mediator at the local mediation center? All options are available in many states. An attorney mediator may be less focused on long-term relationships, and a counselor or community center mediator is probably less knowledgeable about legal issues. If they use a non-attorney mediator, Jean and Sam must consult with their own attorneys about legal issues. If they use an attorney mediator, they may choose to work with a counselor in order to address their relationship issues.

Then, there is the question of Jennifer. The legal system does build in protections for her welfare, but these do not address the turmoil she is experiencing as a consequence of her parents' changing relationship. How will she be prepared for the outcome of the negotiations? Indeed, at age 16, will she have a voice in the negotiations?

Jennifer might have opinions about a number of issues. For example, what limitations will be placed on her parents when it comes to asking Jennifer to carry messages between them? If her parents find new partners, how will they be introduced into her life? There is also the reality that Jennifer's needs may change after the agreement is negotiated. How will her parents work together to make parenting decisions that address these changes, and what role will Jennifer play in those discussions? Jennifer may be invited to express her preferences on some issues, either in mediation or in a counseling session. Including Jennifer increases her sense of having some control over an unstable situation.

Jean and Sam have many options for successfully managing the following strategic challenges.

- Creating a negotiation process or a set of processes that balances and coordinates legal and financial issues with relationship issues.
- Ensuring that Jennifer's needs are taken into account during the negotiation and when they implement the agreement.
- Involving Jennifer in the process in ways that help her adjust to the changes created in her life by her parents' divorce.

The Hard Work of a Corporate Merger

The Acme-Zocon merger and subsequent downsizing of the workforce have introduced instability into the labor-management relationship. Negotiations will probably take place as scheduled, but they are not likely to be routine. The problems associated with developing a new corporate culture, the losses associated with downsizing, and uneven acceptance of the merger within the organization will create problems for the negotiators.

Additionally, the parties must deal with the reality of the global economy. The threat that companies will "exit" their relationship with workers by relocating to other countries has shifted the balance of power between corporations and unions.

In recent decades, many companies have received considerable concessions from workers in order to "preserve their competitive edge while keeping jobs at home." Sometimes these concessions have been won through hard-bargaining tactics that diminished the power of the union or even eliminated the union altogether. Other times concessions have been achieved by shifting the relationship between management and union from adversaries to partners. The latter tactic involves altering identities and telling new relationship stories, much the way Jean and Sam are telling new stories in the process of negotiating their divorce. All of these issues and possibilities loom over the Acme-Zocon negotiations, and they are amplified by the instability created by the merger.

Acme-Zocon management and labor can mitigate the impact of post-merger instability on their negotiations if they acknowledge the full scope of the problems and issues facing the company. To do this, they will need to think quite differently about their agenda and the purpose of their negotiations. Rather than negotiating only over workplace disciplinary procedures and wage and benefit packages, the parties can also think about how they might use this opportunity to address other merger-related problems. Expanding their agenda in this way will require careful information-gathering. Thus the parties might think about conducting a pre-negotiation listening project with middle management and rank-and-file workers to uncover some of the challenges and issues related to merging Acme and Zocon corporate cultures. A listening project could also reveal the level of satisfaction, concern, or discontent arising out of the merger and the layoffs.

Management and labor representatives at Acme-Zocon can use their negotiations strategically to manage the instability in their context if they consider the following challenges:

- Expanding their agenda to accommodate merger-related issues.
- Getting information from the various sectors in the company where the merger is being experienced differently.
- Making their negotiation one part of a larger process to address conflicts arising out of the merger so that Acme-Zocon reaps the full benefits of the merger.

Making Ecosystem Management a Reality

Dialogue processes among ranchers, environmentalists, and federal agency staff have been going on for years in the Southwest. Participants often complain that these dialogues never result in action. Or, the participants think they are negotiating and then one group or the other backs out of the process just as they are about to reach an agreement. This latter problem emerges out of a lack of clarity about the differences between dialogue and negotiation, a lack of careful attention to who is at the table, and failure to ascertain whether those involved are really prepared to negotiate. This demonstrates that great care must be taken in any negotiation to set realistic expectations, clear guidelines for participation, and mechanisms for validating the proceedings as they progress.

The negotiators in our case study are veterans of dialogue projects, relationship-building activities, and confidence-building measures. As a result of participating in these other conflict resolution processes, they now identify themselves as a "radical center" that is ready to "reject the acrimony of past decades that has dominated debate over livestock grazing on public lands, for it has yielded little but hard feelings among people who are united by their common love of land and who should be natural allies."[7] They have chosen to negotiate about a particular site and a limited set of issues: How can we craft an experimental project for cooperatively implementing and monitoring the effects of ecosystem management in this area over the next five to 10 years?

This negotiation requires a delicate balance between caution and hope. The parties need to know that what they are doing here will not impose significant changes in the positions they and other parties not at the table hold about ranching in the Southwest. At the same time, they need to have some hope that lessons learned through this negotiation and the resulting experimental project might yield positive outcomes for what has been an intractable conflict. Limiting the negotiations to a geographically focused land management experiment is the key to getting full participation and buy-in from the parties without falsely inflating hopes or creating a sense of unacceptable risk. Ensuring that the parties are in fact committed to trying something radically new is also important, and this will need attention throughout the negotiation because pressures from other parties will affect the negotiators' calculation of risk and their ongoing commitment to the process.

The balancing act between caution and hope is complicated by identity issues. The participants may be prepared to identify with a radical center, but few of them are ready to sever all of their ties with other groups. They will need those other groups if these negotiations fail, and they need those groups to address the larger conflict over grazing on federally-owned lands. Furthermore, successfully implementing a negotiated agreement may require involving other groups in the experimental project, and it will depend on the ability of the federal agencies to sustain a funding stream and clear mandate for the project over the next five to 10 years. Working with other parties includes communicating clearly about the limitations of the project and creating mechanisms for involving others as negotiations and the experiment progress.

As with many multiparty environmental negotiations, facilitators have been hired to help manage the negotiation. The facilitators can help the parties manage the instability of their context by focusing attention on and helping them develop skills to meet the following challenges:

- Making sure the parties have delineated their agenda and the scope of their negotiations clearly and carefully.
- Helping the parties manage and balance the main negotiations with their behind-the-table negotiations.
- Helping the parties work together across stakeholder group divisions in ways that respect their need to hold positive relationships with others who share their identity (ranchers, environmentalists, etc.).

- Preparing the parties to educate others and involve them in the experimental project once it has been negotiated.
- Helping the parties address the effects of turmoil created by the actions of other parties who are not at the table.

Practical Implications

The parties in our case studies are more likely to succeed in creating and sustaining a negotiation process if they coordinate negotiation with other processes for addressing a conflict. Jean and Sam may want to use a counselor as well as a mediator during their divorce negotiations. Dialogue processes that involve other stakeholders may need to continue alongside negotiations. The parties may agree to negotiate one problem but reserve the right to sue one another over other problems. These limitations should be made as clear as possible when negotiations commence in order to avoid hard feelings and resentment later.

5.
Managing Behind-the-Table Negotiations

In an unstable context, the negotiators' decisions can have far-reaching effects leading other people to take a keen interest in their work. Strategic negotiators learn how to make this outside interest work for the long-term benefit of the negotiated agreement. Rather than seeing "interested outsiders" as a nuisance, good strategic negotiators work with those outsiders to create a constituency that supports the agreement. This constituency is a necessary supplement to or replacement for the institutions that enact and enforce a negotiated agreement in stable settings.

It is helpful to think of strategic negotiation in an unstable context as improvisational theater with a fluid audience, loose rules about participation, and a set that keeps changing. Learning to manage or at least anticipate the actions of parties not at the table is critically important. In an unstable setting, negotiators must pay attention to five types of parties not at the table (see Figure 1, page 14):

- Parties involved in the conflict but represented by others during negotiation.
- Organized parties who share concerns and issues with one or more of the negotiators but who have chosen not to participate in the negotiation.
- Institutions and organizations that may be important for implementing the agreement and may or may not have representatives at the table.
- The unorganized general public whose support for a negotiated agreement may be crucial to its success.
- Powerful external parties not directly involved in the conflict but who can alter the negotiators' BATNA (Best Alternative to a Negotiated Agreement) by changing the context.

This chapter examines some ways that negotiators can manage turbulence introduced into the negotiation by parties they represent. It will also discuss how negotiators might find potential allies in the parties involved in the conflict but who are not at the negotiation table. Chapter 7 will examine ways that negotiators can build and sustain public support for their agreement among the general public and with powerful external parties. But it should be clearly understood that building public support for a negotiated agreement must start right from the

In changing contexts, negotiation can be seen as improvisational theater with a fluid audience, loose rules about participation, and a set that keeps changing.

beginning of the negotiation; it is not simply added on at the end of the process.

Principal-Agent Relationships in Negotiation

When the parties send representatives to the table, the negotiators are "agents" working on behalf of the "principals" in the conflict. The use of agents is a common practice in negotiations, even in stable settings. But an unstable context increases the complexity of the relationships between agents and principals.

Any agreement made by agents must be approved by the principals, which raises questions about reliability. How accurately is each agent representing the interests and positions of his or her party? Can any given agent "deliver" on a negotiated agreement? In other words, will behind-the-table negotiations validate the agreement reached at the negotiation table? Answers to these questions determine the confidence negotiators have in their ability to reach a viable agreement, and this factor influences each party's BATNA (Best Alternative to a Negotiated Agreement).

Answering two questions about each agent at the table can help parties more realistically assess the risk that problems in behind-the-table negotiations will derail the main negotiation:

- How formal and structured is the relationship between this agent and his or her principals?
- How much legitimacy does the agent have?

Using agents need not create turbulence for the negotiators. Some principal-agent relationships are formal and highly structured, as in the case of an attorney hired by a client. The relationship is professional, not personal; it is contractual, not political. Other agents are selected through political processes that may be more or less formal and regulated. For example, an elected union representative keeps a close eye on her constituency so that she will not be turned out of office by the rank-and-file membership. This is a formal and structured process, but it is messier than an attorney-client relationship. Even more messy are relationships between a principal and agent when the party is a loose coalition or voluntary membership group. In groups such as a community association or an ad hoc, issue-specific activist group, membership may fluctuate so that the representative has difficulty presenting a coherent and consistent position. Furthermore, there are few if any formal mechanisms for the group to remove a volunteer agent from the negotiation table.

> In an unstable context, negotiators need to cooperatively build a unified constituency capable of supporting their agreement even while they are negotiating difficult issues with one another.

When the relationship between principal and agent is highly political or informal, it is particularly important to ascertain the agent's legitimacy. Has this agent been chosen in ways that the party considers valid and legal? Does the party believe the agent is doing a credible and acceptable job representing his/her interests and needs? An agent selected through a process deemed fair and appropriate by the party will have higher legitimacy than an agent whose selection was controversial. An agent may also gain legitimacy by succeeding in the negotiation or lose legitimacy by failing. When the party is a group rather than an individual, internal conflicts over the agent's status can disrupt the negotiations, and these should be noted, too.

Taken together, the formality of the agent-principal relationship and the agent's legitimacy with the party help determine the potential for agent-principal conflicts to disrupt inter-party negotiations. Figure 5 illustrates the ways that legitimacy and stability increase or decrease the likelihood that conflicts between a party and its representative will derail a negotiation.[8]

Figure 5
Legitimacy and Formality
of Principal-Agent Relationship

Formal Regulation of Principal-Agent Relationship

I	II
Unstable Principal-Agent relationship but subject to regulation. Disruption of negotiation possible.	Stable Principal-Agent relationship. Regulation possible but not needed. Disruption of negotiation unlikely.
Principal-Agent relationship ranges from unstable to chaotic. Disruption of main negotiation highly likely.	Principal-Agent relationship is stable but subject to changes in political/social context. Disruption of negotiation depends on political developments in the party.
IV	III

Low Legitimacy of Agent — High Legitimacy of Agent

Informal Regulation of Principal-Agent Relationship

The turmoil from the surrounding context can seep into even formal and structured principal-agent relationships. The regulations that govern principal-agent relationships may be questioned or challenged, making it difficult to repair ruptures when they occur. And an unstable context often produces new, loosely-organized stakeholder groups whose principal-agent relationships are particularly difficult to manage. So, during turbulent times, we can expect to see more principal-agent relationships falling into quadrants III and IV on Figure 5.

Some parties càn move quickly while others need significantly more time to approve or reject a proposed agreement. Parties capable of making quick decisions are inclined to think other parties are stalling or negotiating in bad faith. Completing a blank version of the table on pages 53-54 by listing specific parties in a negotiation and their structural characteristics can help negotiators understand the ways the parties' structures affect the negotiation. What feels chaotic becomes understandable and therefore less threatening to the negotiation process.[9]

> One consequence of an unstable negotiating context is high volatility in the principal-agent relationships.

In the New Mexico case, environmentalists, ranchers, and agency staff all act as agents but for very different types of principals. The agency staff can probably speak most confidently for their principals, but the agencies are not a single entity. They compete for resources and prestige, and both agencies are vulnerable to changes in the political arena. The environmental advocates at the table may work with highly-structured nonprofit organizations; in this case their ability to deliver on agreements is similar to that of the federal agency representatives. Other environmental representatives are probably speaking on behalf of more loosely-organized local environmental advocates that are more like neighborhood associations. Here, their ability to deliver on an agreement is more

Figure 6
Negotiation Parties
and Their Social Structure

Type of party	Nature of structure	Speed with which it can act	Coherence of goals
Corporation	Highly organized; hierarchical.	Quickly—once the necessary component parts become involved.	Very coherent—clear, widely-shared standards for measuring success (i.e., bottom line).
Union	Highly organized; political.	Moderately quickly once a proposal is up for a vote, *unless* there is political turmoil in the union.	Usually coherent, but may be less coherent in times of rapid system change.
Advocacy Groups	Range from highly organized, with paid staff to serve as agents, to loosely organized, with volunteers to act as agents.	Range from moderately quickly to slowly and uncertainly.	Range from clear, single-agenda goals, to clearly articulated concerns but unclear markers for achieving success.

Type of party	Nature of structure	Speed with which it can act	Coherence of goals
Government Agency	Hierarchical. Organized, but may have some incoherence in the system due to competing mandates and the influence of political actors on policies and standard operating procedures.	Slowly, compared to corporations. Quickly, compared to community organizations and other political groups	May be confused by competing mandates and shifting political scene.
Community Organization — e.g., Neighborhood Association	Semi-structured. Democratic and therefore open to change.	Relatively slowly — needs time to build consensus through democratic processes.	May not be fully coherent because of multiple competing goals. May lack shared standards for measuring success.
Nondominant cultural group Example used here: Native American Tribe [Note: What is needed here is a cultural analysis of the group's decision-making style.]	Frequently subject to internal conflicts between "progressive" and "traditional" factions. Culturally more likely to work by consensus rather than by majority vote.	May be very slow, particularly if tribe works by consensus and deliberation.	May be difficult to discern because of internal conflicts.

tenuous. The ranchers are probably the least organized of the negotiators. Participants negotiate on their own behalf as local ranchers with a significant stake in the outcome, but they also speak as self-nominated representatives for "progressive ranchers." They may have few mechanisms for ascertaining whether other local ranchers will accept a negotiated agreement.

If the parties acknowledge and address these behind-the-table factors during negotiation, they can set more realistic expectations about how quickly a proposed agreement can be ratified or rejected. They can also increase the possibility of a successful outcome by helping each other figure out what kind of agreement they can each "sell" to their principals.

In the Acme-Zocon case, the parties should be aware that normally routine affirmation of a negotiated agreement may not be easy to achieve. Management and labor may both be in disarray as a result of the merger, thus slowing down their ability to ratify an agreement. Furthermore, if the "shadow" issues of merging corporate cultures, coping with downsizing, and residual "we-they" identities are not addressed at the negotiation table, the proposed agreement may become the battleground where the principals express their anxiety and dissatisfaction with the turmoil in their context.

Structuring Negotiations with Agents and Principals

When agents are negotiating on behalf of principals, they must consult with their constituencies during negotiation. If some of the parties are not well organized, or if they are operating with cultural norms about consultation that require lengthy deliberation, the timeframe for negotiation must be adjusted accordingly. It will be tempting for the more streamlined groups to push others to operate as efficiently as they do. However, forcing the agents to work without adequate consultation with their principals is a big mistake. The issues that are overlooked through forced efficiency will come back to haunt the parties at the time of final ratification.

Working with Stakeholders Who Decline to Negotiate

Organized parties with a stake in the conflict who do not join negotiations can be seen as a threat to the process or as a potential asset for promoting system changes that deal with underlying, deep-rooted conflicts. In reality, they are both. They have the potential to undercut any agreement. They are organized and they care enough about the issues to protest a settlement they deem wrong or unwise. These groups can also influence the general public. Consequently, in unstable situations, we often see ad hoc, issue-specific groups forming quickly to protest and prevent implementation of agreements that others may have worked years to craft.

> The organized parties not at the table may be the key to creating systems that support a negotiated agreement.

Negotiators can avoid this if they treat other organized groups as potential allies and helpful sources of feedback for testing proposed agreements. They can gather information from stakeholder groups through formal or informal conversations. By engaging other parties, the negotiators can demonstrate that they are taking the concerns of others seriously, test likely reactions to proposed solutions, keep the door open for others to join negotiations, and prepare others to support and implement agreements later.

This strategic approach to negotiating in an unstable context is best accomplished if the negotiators decide jointly how to gather information from other parties. They need to pay close attention to:

- Allotting adequate time for consultations with other groups.
- Deciding when and how to consult with others.
- Reaching a shared agreement regarding what information about their negotiations will be shared with others.

As with principal-agent relationships, the time required for consultation with other stakeholder groups will depend, in part, on the structure of those groups, the speed with which they can act, and the coherence of their goals. (See chart on pages 53-54.) By assessing the situation together, negotiators can better calculate the time needed for consultations. To preserve confidentiality, the negotiators can make joint decisions about when and how they will share information with others. This includes deciding how to balance informal and more formal consultations, whether to present their ideas jointly or separately, and how to decide what information is ready to be shared.

Informal consultations occur naturally. For example, in the ecosystem management case, ranchers might discuss issues related to ecosystem management with fellow members of the local cattlemen's association, while agency representatives discuss similar issues at staff meetings or professional gatherings. Informal feedback is helpful, but gathering it entails risks that need to be managed. Negotiators might only hear what already confirms their own view, and they might unconsciously present a distorted version of the ideas being considered by the negotiators. They can also unintentionally increase tensions among the parties if they share information in ways that damage some negotiators' standing with other stakeholder groups.

To check the validity of informally-gathered information, negotiators can convene more formal meetings such as public feedback sessions with a cross-section of stakeholders.[10] When doing this, negotiators should think carefully about how to share information in ways that don't incite resistance to the negotiation process. A facilitator with no stake in the negotiation can help structure the information-sharing and -gathering process to elicit open-ended, creative, and non-judgmental responses. Using a facilitator also allows the negotiators to listen attentively to the participants' ideas. A further benefit of public meetings for multiple stakeholder groups is the way they create space for parties not involved in formal negotiations to converse with others who do not share their views. This provides a rare and precious opportunity for people to renegotiate their shared lives when old ways of managing their interactions are in turmoil.

> Negotiators need to think carefully about how to share information in ways that don't incite resistance to the process.

Practical Implications

When trying to balance behind-the-table negotiations with the negotiations at the table, negotiators may have difficulty allocating their time and energy between the two processes. They may become impatient with the way working with other parties slows down their negotiations. Thinking of themselves as a temporary "learning organization"[11] as well as negotiators can help the negotiators balance at-the-table and behind-the-table negotiations. When they are problem-solving or bargaining, they can focus on negotiating. When they want to test a possible agreement, they would do well to become a learning team that works cooperatively to gather and assess information. Being clear about when and how they switch between these roles is helpful.

6.
Negotiating
Meaning

Why all this fuss about people who are not at the negotiation table? What makes it so difficult to pin down the actors, the scene, and the set for negotiation in turbulent times? Why can't we just impose control on the negotiation process, limit the participation to willing parties, and ignore those who choose not to participate?

Negotiating the Context

The answer lies in Figure 2 (page 20). As we saw in Chapter 3, to negotiate issues the parties need to have a coordinated or shared sense of their context. In stable times, the shared sense of reality is enacted through institutions such as the courts, the schools, the political system, local elders, and bureaucracies. In times of turbulence, which are often brought on by changes that destabilize existing social systems, the parties do not share a sense of their context adequate to support negotiation. The structures that create a shared sense of meaning may be broken or missing; they can no longer function because they do not have adequate support from the citizenry or because they literally have been destroyed.

Missing or broken systems cannot be imposed; they must be renegotiated and revalidated by the people, and this is a challenge of meaning-making. In each of our three case studies, the context of negotiations is unstable in large measure because the parties give different meanings to their shared environment and to their relationships. Some people talk about parties in conflict having different perceptions or different worldviews. Perceptions and worldviews are not the same thing, and the differences between them are important.

> Worldview differences are often root causes of conflict. They require careful attention to the ways people construct their senses of reality.

The girls negotiating to divide the orange in Chapter 2 perceived the orange differently; one girl valued the orange for its peel while the other valued its fruit and juice. Both girls treated the orange as a useful commodity suitable for bargaining or trading. If one girl had seen the orange as a sacred object that should not be harmed and the other had seen it as a commodity to be traded, we would say they had different worldviews because they gave different *meaning* to the orange.

Perception differences can usually be addressed through gathering or sharing information, which is how the mother helped the girls recognize that they both could have what they wanted of the orange. Worldview differences are more difficult. Such differences require careful attention to the ways people construct their senses of reality.

It is helpful to think about people as *worldviewing* beings. Worldviewing is an active process of meaning-making that shapes our sense of reality and our understanding of our options for action. Everyone engages in worldviewing, but our worldviewing activities are largely unconscious, and our own worldview is such "common sense" to us that we see it only when we encounter someone who does not share our "common sense."

We cannot easily answer the question, "What is your worldview?" but our worldviews are revealed in our language and behaviors. They are particularly evident in the stories we tell about our lives and the world around us. In our storytelling and our actions, we indirectly answer five questions:

- What is real?
- How is the world organized?
- What do we value and devalue about the world?
- What constitutes real knowledge about the world?
- How should we (and others) act in the world?

Worldviews are not infinitely malleable, but neither are they fixed and immutable. They contain uncertainties and internal inconsistencies, and they change in response to shifting circumstances, including encounters with others who do not share the same worldview. Remember Bobby's mother in Chapter 2? She changed her sense of reality and her understanding of how she should act in order to negotiate with Bobby about his school clothes. Her worldviewing changes were necessary to create the context for negotiation.

Unstable settings expose the uncertainties, inconsistencies, and conflicts in the parties' worldviewing, and this forces them to expend energy on making sense of the five worldviewing questions listed above. Therefore, they must spend more time than usual on storytelling and other activities that help them create a sense of reality that is adequately shared to allow for joint action in the world, including the joint action of negotiation.

In many unstable settings, the parties' competing senses of reality are among the root causes of their conflict. For example, Jean may unconsciously think about marriage as a shared journey in which partners support one another through life changes, while Sam may see it as a contract with clearly spelled out roles and expectations. This makes her return to school and all of the change that has brought to their home life and their relationship problematic for him and a natural progression of life for her. They may not even recognize this difference until they start telling their stories in the presence of another person who can help them explore the meaning they attach to their lives.

> In an unstable context, negotiators must make room for storytelling in order to negotiate the reality in which they are trying to live together.

Parties in a conflict may even do worldviewing in ways that exclude or make invisible some parts of reality, including parties who are involved in the conflict! For example, some environmentalists assume that human beings are not part of "natural" ecosystems; they are inherently detrimental to fragile landscapes such as desert rangeland. Therefore, the rural communities that depend on the land are either invisible to environmentalists or they are identified as the problem. In similar fashion, some ranchers dismiss ecosystems as mere fancy talk, a ploy by environmentalists to destroy ranching as a lifestyle. Self-identified progressive ranchers, by contrast, claim that bad ranching practices have caused damage to the rangelands. They see ecosystems as real, but they argue that human communities are part of the ecosystem and good ranching practices can improve ecosystem health. At the core of this conflict are worldviewing questions: Are ecosystems real? If yes, are human communities that live off the land part of the ecosystem, or are they an unnatural intruder into the ecosystem? An interest-based negotiation process alone cannot create space for the parties to explore this worldviewing problem.

In unstable settings, the parties need to identify and wrestle with their worldviewing differences in order to create a sense of a shared reality that can sustain new relationships and new ways of living together. The traditional rational-analytical processes of negotiation and the instrumental and relational language of negotiation are not adequate for shared meaning-making. Stories must be told, listened to deeply, and new shared stories must be created if the parties are going to stabilize a sense of reality that accommodates a peaceful future.

Making Room for Storytelling in Negotiation

Storytelling enters any negotiation when the parties use persuasion to make their case for a particular agreement. Party A says, "Because the world is this way and our relationship is like this, then you *should* do X." Party B counters with an alternate story about reality and a different suggested outcome. In spite of this, few negotiation guides focus on the nature of the stories people tell during negotiation and the way these stories shape the negotiation process. And little attention has been given to the ways negotiators can combine processes of shared storytelling (renegotiating reality) and problem-solving (negotiating issues).

Divorce mediation (assisted negotiation) is one practice that often makes room for the parties to share their stories. This may happen during mediation, or the couple may work on retelling their stories with a counselor and coordinate renegotiating their reality in counseling with negotiating the legal and technical details of their divorce in mediation. The stories crafted in the counseling sessions shape the negotiations in the mediation session. If a divorce mediator is also a counselor, he may weave these processes together rather than sending the couple to another counselor.

Complex multiparty negotiations such as "Making Ecosystem Management a Reality" may be preceded by or accompanied by processes for building positive relationships among the parties. This creates some opportunity to negotiate reality, but the possibilities are limited since meaning-making is about more than just building positive relationships; it is also about building a shared story about the world that can include all of the parties in ways they find meaningful and appropriate. For example, one usually unspoken story that influences environmental negotiation is

> Negotiating effectively in an unstable context requires increased awareness of the types of stories people tell when they are in conflict and the potential pitfalls as well as the benefits of focusing on stories during negotiation.

the story of human beings as managers of the natural world. This story makes it difficult to raise issues of values, ethics, and meaning that might envision another relationship between nature and human communities. The parties can spend time together and build positive interpersonal relationships, but if they don't focus on creating a story that embraces other possible relationships between human beings and nature, they will have a hard time negotiating intractable environmental conflicts.

The lack of attention to storytelling in negotiation is unfortunate. The dividing line between negotiating reality and negotiating issues is never clear and bright. The processes are necessarily intertwined because there is great power associated with the process of "naming the reality" of a relationship. In stable settings the reality is named by the institutions and relationships that are recognized as legitimate by the parties. That shared or created reality establishes and sustains the context for negotiation. In unstable settings, the contest over naming reality is as important as—or possibly more important than—the particular issues being negotiated.

World-Naming Power and Storytelling

Even if we acknowledge the importance of meaning-making in negotiation, it is not always easy to include storytelling in ways that are fair and helpful. The greatest power in any relationship is the power to name reality and entice, coerce, or persuade others to live inside the reality we have named. In negotiation, there is a risk that one party will impose a story that prevents the other party from speaking his or her sense of reality. This risk is greatly increased when the parties tell their stories sequentially because the second narrator can easily become trapped in the story told by the first narrator.

Let's assume that the mediators ask Jean to tell her story about the divorce first, and she says:

> We are getting a divorce, because Sam started an affair with his secretary after I went back to school in order to resume my career when Jennifer goes to college. He clearly does not want me to develop my own career. Things would have been fine for him if I continued to be a stay-at-home wife...if I were always there to meet his needs rather than think about what I need to be happy and healthy. He obviously feels threatened by my growing independence and he prefers the company of his new girlfriend who admires him and focuses all her energy on him.

Sam is already put in a low power position, because he must use his storytelling opportunity to counter the negative images in Jean's story. Given the cultural stereotypes of successful men trading in first wives for younger trophy wives, Sam must also counter the negative images that Jean's story conjures from the surrounding culture.

Consider how differently negotiations might unfold if Sam told his story first and said:

> I don't understand why we are getting a divorce. Things were fine. Then Jean said she wanted to go back to school and resume her career. I tried to be supportive, but nothing I do seems to be enough for her. She seems so angry about having stayed home to raise Jennifer, so

angry about the support she gave me in my career. I come home and she is not there; she is out at some meeting or with her study group. I want to go away for a long weekend like we used to do, but she has to write a paper. Nothing is the same. We don't have a marriage anymore, because Jean has "checked out" of our marriage.

The power associated with telling the story of a shifting relationship, as in the case of a divorce, has serious implications for negotiating legal and financial settlements. If the mediators and Jean consciously or unconsciously shape the reality within which issues will be decided using Jean's story, they diminish Sam's capacity to make claims related to financial resources. They and even he may think he needs to "pay" for his wrongdoing. If, on the other hand, the mediators and Sam consciously or unconsciously shape the reality using a story that portrays Jean as having betrayed the unspoken rules of her relationship with Sam, then she is put at a disadvantage. Sam, the mediators, and even Jean may assume that the "cost" of her independence is a diminished right to make claims on Sam for support.

Similar problems exist in all of our cases. If Acme is portrayed as rescuing Zocon from poor management practices, then persons, practices, and policies associated with Zocon will be disadvantaged in formal or informal negotiations to enact the merger. The ecosystem management parties can't negotiate if the ranchers think of all environmentalists as "city-dwelling tree-huggers" who know nothing about living on the land, and if the environmentalists think all ranchers are "bad guys" who care nothing about the environment. They must embrace a story in which they each give up a part of their own righteous self-identity.

Negotiated Agreements Are World-Naming Stories

A negotiated agreement is a world-naming story; it embodies new ways of talking about and acting in the world and it accepts a limited array of possible relationships among parties. As with any world-naming story, it can exclude or include others. Because all of the parties involved are not at the table, the negotiators can easily fall into a trap of creating a shared narrative that displaces the blame for their current situation and loads the cost of fixing the problem onto someone not in the negotiation. Negotiators need to remember that the parties they are blaming are part of the "audience" that needs to validate and support the agreement. Therefore, displacing the blame for the problem and the burden for fixing it is a recipe for failure.

Even if blame is not displaced, others will experience the world-naming story of a negotiated agreement as an attempt to reshape their reality and control their options in life. They may embrace this story, or they may reject it, particularly if they are not "in" the story or if they think enacting the story will cause harm to them or to things and people they cherish. Their resistance can take the form of lawsuits,

> In an unstable setting, negotiators can maximize their potential for success if they recognize and embrace their opportunity to help the wider system stabilize around a new shared story.

protests, media campaigns, or even violence.

As discussed in the previous chapter, consulting with stakeholders not at the table can prevent the negotiation of an agreement (the creation of a world-naming story) that incites resistance from key groups. More difficult to manage is the way the general public will respond to a proposed agreement. Negotiators can work with this challenge by altering their self-identity. In the last chapter, I suggested that negotiators also need to become a learning organization in order to work with parties not at the table. They also need to think of themselves as community leaders, particularly when they look ahead to getting an agreement approved and implemented. In times of crisis or instability, effective community leaders help people articulate a new vision and move effectively toward making that vision real. The next chapter looks at ways negotiators can build support for their agreement.

> It may be important to consult with stakeholders not at the table. Negotiators may need to think of themselves as community leaders.

Practical Implications

Moving back and forth between storytelling and problem-solving can be difficult. Storytelling about the past is one part of the process, but there is also a need to play with and envision new stories for the future. These new stories direct attention to the context and the way the negotiated agreement will affect the context for good or for ill. Negotiators need to play with and explore answers to questions such as these: If we agree to "X," what will our future look like? Who will need to be involved? How will it feel? What will this allow us to do? What will it prevent us from doing? How will it affect others? Is it sustainable? Is this new way of being together in keeping with our community values? Does this agreement reshape the world in ways that are positive and beneficial?

When doing this kind of exploration, it is helpful if the negotiators can carve out a time and place for the free flow of creativity without judgment or risk of getting trapped into an agreement or commitment. This can be done with brainstorming sessions, visioning activities, role-playing (parties take on the roles of others in the conflict), and other creative learning activities. It is useful to mark these times clearly as "not negotiating" so that the parties participate freely and creatively. Literally moving to a different location and setting the furniture in the room differently can help free participants from the mind-set of negotiating. Getting a facilitator to help with the process can also change the parties' understanding of what they are doing. The key to success, however, is finding ways to engage participants in creative conversations, or what Stephen Littlejohn calls "transcendent communication," that invites the participants to shift the way they view themselves, others, and their problem.[12]

7.
Mobilizing and Sustaining Support for the Agreement

Let's assume the negotiators in each of our three cases have reached an agreement. Now what happens? That depends on the support systems that exist and on the support that negotiators can win from those who were not involved in the negotiation. If support systems are missing or lack legitimacy, then the negotiators will need to sell the agreement to others. This is not an either/or situation; rather, it is a matter of degree. Even if support mechanisms such as the courts are fully functional, the parties may need to build political support so that other parties don't prevent the ratification and implementation of the negotiated agreement. Let's look at our three cases.

Thus far we have addressed Jean and Sam's negotiations as though Jennifer were the only other party they need to consider. This may not be entirely accurate. Legally they are responsible only for Jennifer, but cultural or family norms may bring other people into the picture when they enact the divorce agreement. It is important to note that the case of Jean and Sam makes many cultural assumptions and reflects dominant-culture attitudes toward marriage and divorce.

In a multicultural society, many families have cultural assumptions about marriage that would require involving extended family members in the divorce negotiation from the beginning. Even in families that don't expect extended family to be involved in divorce negotiations, Jennifer's adjustment to the divorce may be easier if extended family members cooperate with and speak positively about the agreement between Jean and Sam. Perhaps Jean and Sam belong to religious communities that have their own legal proceedings or rituals for ending a marriage. In other words, if Jean and Sam need or want others to support their agreement, they must negotiate for that support.

> Negotiators may have to sell the agreement to those not involved in the negotiations.

The Acme-Zocon negotiators can rely on institutional supports for their agreement, but those supports may be limited or fragile. If they have used this round of negotiations to address issues arising from merging corporate cultures, they may need to garner unusual types of support and resources to implement the agreement. Let's say, for example, that they have agreed to general guidelines for workplace discipline, but they are also proposing that workers and managers participate in a facilitated process to talk about blending the cultural norms of Acme and Zocon. They also want to establish an oversight committee to monitor and evaluate the effectiveness of the new disciplinary process and make necessary adjustments prior to their next round of bargaining. They need resources for the facilitated meetings and the monitoring project, and they need political support from workers and management to ratify an agreement that is less definitive than normal.

The negotiators in the rangeland management case have designed a learning activity that requires the creation and maintenance of long-term relationships organized around a multi-year experiment in ecosystem management. They need other parties either to support the project or, at a minimum, to remain neutral long enough for the experiment to be conducted and evaluated. They must marshal the resources to conduct the experiment in a manner that will produce widely validated results. They may even want parties not involved in the negotiation to help with data-gathering and data analysis, or they may want them to serve as an oversight committee for the project.

> Negative responses to an agreement may be expressions of frustration at a chaotic world.

Carrying out the agreement in this case relies heavily on the ability of the federal agencies to sustain a commitment to the project. Since Congress controls their budgets and their policy directions are set by political appointees, the agencies are indirectly influenced by the will of the public. If the general public mobilizes against the project, Congress or the agency directors can end the project. This is a case where wooing public support is particularly important, but the negotiators may not see that clearly.

Understanding Why Others Resist the Agreement

Having worked hard to craft an agreement on difficult issues, negotiators are frequently surprised when others resist their proposed plans, and they often are unprepared to manage the negative responses. Before doubting the merits of their work or getting angry with others for being uncooperative, negotiators must consider the environment in which they are working. Negative responses may not be a reactions to the proposal as much as they are expressions of frustration with a world that feels chaotic.

There is much evidence that change and social conflict go hand-in-hand. Since change destabilizes the existing social order, some people benefit from change while others suffer from the same change. In many cases, people don't know whether they will benefit or suffer from change; they just find it uncomfortable. Or they assume that they will be the losers rather than the beneficiaries of change.

The negotiators have reclaimed a sense of control over their lives through the negotiation process. Others have not shared their experience. Consequently, when the negotiators enthusiastically introduce their proposal, others may only hear that yet another change is being thrust upon them.

The following factors influence the way people respond to change:

- Did they choose the change or was it imposed on them?
- Did they anticipate the change or was it unexpected?
- Is the change seen as a minor inconvenience or a major disruptive force?
- Does the change feel positive or negative to them?

If negotiators understand and work with these realities, they can introduce the changes they are proposing in ways that maximize the potential for support.

Anticipating, Preventing, and Working with Public Resistance

The previous chapter described ways the negotiators can work with other stakeholder groups to make sure their agreement considers a broad array of interests and needs. But what about people not tied to stakeholder groups? Do they need to be considered in strategic negotiations?

In unstable settings, the negotiators lack the capacity and legitimacy to make others cooperate with their plans, and the institutions that might otherwise enforce an agreement are too unstable to fulfill that role. Therefore, the negotiators must take responsibility for building the political will and, wherever possible, the institutional mechanisms for supporting and sustaining newly negotiated cooperative relationships. Exactly how much an agreement depends on political support from the public must be determined case by case. In some situations, just getting the public not to protest or resist an agreement is adequate. In other situations, the public must actively cooperate to implement the agreement.

Finding the balance between sharing information and creating the space for negotiators to take risks and be creative is a delicate process

Secrecy is antithetical to the slow process of building political will. But many negotiators think that secrecy is necessary to get their work done, and they are right in some ways. You can't do hard negotiating and problem-solving with television cameras tracking your every move. In strategic negotiations, finding the balance between sharing information to prepare the public for an agreement and creating the space for negotiators to take risks and be creative is a delicate process.

When thinking about how much information to share with the public, negotiators should consider two factors:

- How significantly will the negotiated outcome affect the general public?
- How much public support will be necessary to implement the negotiated agreement?

Preparing the Public

To find the balance between secrecy and transparency, the negotiators need a shared map of the overall situation. Before they even begin discussing particular problems or issues, they can use Figure 1 (page 14) and Figure 4 (page 34) as templates for identifying other actors. Even if they do not reach complete agreement on this map, they can still use it to make plans for managing the behind-the-table interactions needed to support their work. They can also revisit the map periodically to make sense of contextual changes that develop during their negotiations.

As they build their map and later as they craft an agreement, the negotiators need to think about how much public support will be required to implement their agreement. Does their agreement need voter approval? Does it need citizen cooperation? Does it expect people to change their behaviors? Does it simply need public tolerance rather than active support? Does it require the support of powerful actors such as Congress and the president in the rangeland case?

While working through problems and building support among organized stakeholder groups not at the table, the negotiators should also think about how much information they need to share with the public, when to share the information, and how best to share it. The more changes a negotiated agreement demands of the general public, the more transparent the negotiations need to be. People change more readily if they understand why a change is needed and if they feel they had some input into the ways the change will be implemented. Similarly, the more the agreement depends on active support from the public, the more the negotiators need to educate and prepare the public to understand the agreement.

Educating the public requires much more than periodic announcements that the negotiations are going well or floating proposed agreements to see how the public responds. Strategies negotiators might consider for keeping the public informed about their work include:

- Have stakeholder groups not at the table educate their constituents about the positive work being done.
- Get normally hostile stakeholder groups to make a joint statement of support for the negotiation process.
- Prepare joint press releases about the negotiation and invite feedback from the public.
- Make sure the general public is aware of public feedback meetings and structure those meetings so that persons not tied to stakeholder groups can participate.

- Invite media to do in-depth stories about the issues to increase public awareness of the problems the negotiators are addressing.

When anticipating public responses to their agreement, negotiators should give careful consideration to the problems that arise when changes threaten people's identities. Conflict feels chaotic to people, but a sustained conflict develops a stability of its own. Institutions and organizations form around the conflict and derive their purpose from the conflict. Individuals and groups begin to derive their identities in opposition to an "enemy other." Thus, positive changes in relationships can actually be very threatening to people and organizations. Implementing positive changes is a long, difficult process of reshaping organizations and institutions and helping people find new ways of defining a positive self-identity that does not rely on an oppositional enemy.

> The more changes a negotiated agreement demands of the general public, the more transparent the negotiations need to be.

Being Realistic About the Agreement

After long and difficult negotiations, the negotiators may be both exhausted and elated. In celebrating their success, they run the risk of over-selling the agreement by saying or implying that all will now be well; the peace was won. The people may celebrate with them but quickly become disillusioned by the normal and inevitable setbacks in implementing the agreement.

The negotiators are also tired. They probably don't have the energy to implement the agreement, and they are often not the correct people for that job. If they have done their work well and brought others into the negotiation as consultants or shadow negotiators, they can hand the process of executing the agreement to others. At the same time, the negotiators, or perhaps another oversight group created as part of the negotiated agreement, need to be prepared to revisit issues and renegotiate unanticipated problems as they arise.

Mobilizing Resources

Implementing agreements in complex cases is a long-term undertaking that involves mobilizing resources and coordinating the activities of multiple organizations and actors. Of our three case studies, only Jean and Sam appear to be in control of the resources needed to implement their agreement. Everyone else will need support of various types from parties not in the primary negotiation. The more a settlement depends on resources not controlled by the parties at the table, the greater the need for negotiators to work throughout their process on behind-the-table negotiations to mobilize those resources. Creating a shared vision and shared realistic plans for mobilizing resources is an important part of strategic negotiation in unstable settings.

> Negotiators need to think about cultivating visionary leadership at all levels of the system.

Cultivating Visionary Leadership

When there are few stable institutions to support a negotiated agreement, visionary leadership is critically important. Keeping in mind the lesson from Acme-Zo-con (Figure 3, page 29), negotiators need to think about cultivating visionary leadership at all levels of the system in which they are working. Again, this is part of the behind-the-table negotiation process during negotiation, and it is a significant factor in the success of an agreement.

The biggest challenge here is creating a sense of shared leadership. In times of turmoil, people often look for strong leaders who can "fix things." Insofar as the negotiators have taken on the role of community leaders in order to cultivate support for the agreement, others may want them to remain in leadership roles or assume more responsibility for the long-term success of the agreement than is realistic or appropriate. If the negotiators have identified leaders throughout the system, invited them into the negotiation process through behind-the-table consultations, and garnered their support for the agreement, then the negotiators can feel more confident that others will put energy into making the agreement a reality.

Introducing and Explaining the Agreement

When introducing their agreement, negotiators need to be clear about what they have and have not negotiated. Otherwise, many people will expect more than is realistic from the agreement. They should also help people understand how this small agreement will help promote long-term changes for the better. Here, the negotiators do well to remember that they are inviting people into a new story; they are not presenting a list of rational, logical steps that people will follow because they make sense. People act out of their stories more than their sense of logic. They need to see and feel how this agreement opens new possibilities for a better life.

James Laue, who taught at the George Mason University Conflict Analysis and Resolution Program, often said, "You can resolve any conflict if you don't care who gets the credit." This is a hard piece of wisdom to follow when you have dedicated immense amounts of time and energy to a negotiation. But in an unstable setting, this can make or break the success of an agreement. Negotiators should ponder carefully who makes the announcement of the agreement. Clearly, they need to own their work. But their work may have a better chance of succeeding if they share the limelight with others less involved in the negotiation, particularly if they can get a coalition of normally-hostile groups who were not at the table to stand with them in support of the agreement.

Planning for Resiliency

The turbulent context means that any negotiated agreement is going to encounter difficulties and setbacks. Negotiators can prepare for this by building into their agreement mechanisms for revisiting the agreement when problems occur. For example, in the Acme-Zocon case and the ecosystem management case, the negotiators created oversight teams, including teams that involve others not at the table. When presenting the agreement, the fact that setbacks will occur should be openly acknowledged. Then when the first problem happens, the negotiators can help immensely if they stand united in their commitment to the agreement, normalize the difficulties, and provide leadership for getting through the problem.

Conclusion

Obviously, negotiating in an unstable context is a difficult and complicated endeavor. I hope this book has pointed to some of the ways negotiators can be successful even in turbulent times, and can help negotiators bring about positive social changes in the midst of what feels like chaos to many people.

Strategic Negotiation Checklist

The following checklist captures some of the special features of strategic negotiation. Chapter and figure numbers direct the reader to discussions of each issue in this book. This is not an exhaustive checklist of the entire negotiation process.

Preparing to Negotiate. Other conflict resolution processes can be used to help parties determine whether to negotiate, who will come to the table, and what they are willing to negotiate. Dialogue groups allow people to build positive relationships and explore issues without any pressure to reach an agreement. Joint problem analysis helps parties reach a commonly-held definition of their problems. And, visioning processes can help the parties think about an ideal future that might accommodate all of their needs. This can also help the parties identify a shared goal before they negotiate specific issues. *When moving into negotiation, don't forget to:*

- Meet the preconditions for negotiation (Chapter 2).
- Use confrontational tactics with care (Chapter 2).

- Think strategically about the forum for negotiation (Chapter 3).
- Clearly mark the transition from dialogue or other activities to negotiation (Chapter 4, ecosystem case).
- Decide whether to use a mediator or facilitator (Chapter 4).
- Calculate your BATNA (Chapter 4).

Negotiating Strategically. The following activities address the big picture that separates strategic from tactical negotiations. *When negotiating strategically, remember to:*

- Identify the sources of instability in your situation (Chapter 3).
- Work together to make the forum serve negotiations; don't squeeze negotiations into an existing forum (Chapter 3).
- Make shared maps of the actors in the wider context (Chapters 5, 7; Figures 1, 4, 5 & Table in Chapter 5).
- Help each other manage behind-the-table negotiations (Chapter 5).
- Keep the negotiation open to information from others involved in the conflict (Chapters 5, 7) .
- Make the negotiators a "learning team" when gathering information from others (Chapter 5).
- Set realistic time lines for consultation with others not at the table (Chapter 5).
- Prepare others for the agreement (Chapters 5, 7).
- Check proposed agreements against the needs and concerns of others not at the table (Chapters 5, 6, 7).
- Plan ahead for implementation (Chapter 7).
- Find a balance between transparency and secrecy (Chapter 7).

- Act as community leaders not just self-interested negotiators (Chapters 6, 7).
- Coordinate negotiation with other conflict resolution activities (Chapters 3, 5, 6).

Negotiating Meaning: The following activities address the need to create new meaning in times of turmoil. *When negotiating strategically, remember to:*

- Combine problem-solving activities and creative meaning-making activities at the table and behind the table (Chapters 2, 6, 7).
- Invite others into the process of making new meaning (Chapter 6).
- Prepare others for the world-naming story of the agreement (Chapters 6, 7).
- Avoid a world-naming story that places all of the blame onto others not at the table (Chapter 6).
- Share the story and not just the technical details of the agreement when bringing it out to the public (Chapter 7).

Implementing the Agreement. The agreement is only the beginning of the process of bringing stability to an unstable setting. *Strategic negotiators are more effective when they:*

- Plan ahead for implementation (Chapter 7).
- Negotiate for support from others not at the table (Chapters 5, 6, 7).
- Cultivate visionary leadership throughout the system (Chapter 7).

- Prepare themselves and others for setbacks (Chapter 7).
- Build mechanisms into the agreement for revisiting negotiations (Chapter 7).

Endnotes

1 (New York: The Free Press, 1986), 1.

2 These three cases are fictionalized composites of cases. "Making Ecosystem Management a Reality," comes closest to being an actual case; it is based, in part, on research conducted by Murl Baker during his practicum with the Conflict Transformation Program at Eastern Mennonite University.

3 Figure 2 is adapted from Jayne Seminare Docherty, *Learning Lessons from Waco: When the Parties Bring Their Gods to the Negotiation Table* (Syracuse, NY: Syracuse University Press, 2001).

4 This book is too small to address the processes used to create the conditions for negotiation in any detail. For more information on this, see Lisa Schirch, *The Little Book of Strategic Peacebuilding* (Intercourse, PA: Good Books, 2004), and Jennifer Gerarda Brown et al., "Negotiation as One of Many Tools," *Marquette Law Review* 87 (2004): 853-860.

5 Figure 3 is adapted from John Paul Lederach, *Building Peace: Sustainable Reconciliation in Divided Societies* (United States Institute of Peace Press, 1997).

6 See http://www.beyondintractability.org/m/conflict_assessment.jsp and http://www.mediate.com/articles/assessment.cfm for descriptions of conflict assessments as they are conducted by third-party intervenors. The same techniques can be used by negotiators themselves.

7 See http://www.quiviracoalition.org/documents/invitation.asp.

8 An earlier version of Figure 5 appeared in Jayne Seminare Docherty and Marcia Caton Campbell, "Teach-

ing Negotiators to Analyze Conflict Structure and Anticipate the Consequences of Principal-Agent Relationships,"
Marquette Law Review 87 (2004): 661.

9 An earlier version of this table appeared in Jayne
Seminare Docherty and Marcia Caton Campbell, "Teach-
ing Negotiators to Analyze Conflict Structure and Anticipate the Consequences of Principal-Agent Relationships,"
Marquette Law Review 87 (2004): 663.

10 For a comparative study of nine attempts to incorporate different types of consultation processes into a de-
cision-making negotiation, see Martha Brand, "Consen-
sus Building and 'Smart Growth,'" *Conflict Resolution
Quarterly* 21 (2003): 189-209.

11 See http://www.breakoutofthebox.com/learning.htm.

12 See Stephen W. Littlejohn, "The Transcendent Communication Project: Searching for a Praxis of Dialogue,"
and Susan O'Malley Wade, "Using Intentional, Values-
Based Dialogue to Engage Complex Public Policy Conflicts," both in *Conflict Resolution Quarterly* 21 (2004): 337-
359 and 361-379. While these papers focus on multiparty
stakeholder dialogues, similar communication techniques
can also be applied to interpersonal and organizational negotiations.

About the Author

Jayne Seminare Docherty is an associate professor of conflict studies in Eastern Mennonite University's Center for Justice and Peacebuilding. She is the author of *Learning Lessons from Waco: When the Parties Bring Their Gods to the Negotiation Table* and various papers in journals such as *Nova Religio* and *Terrorism and Political Violence*. She is also author or co-author of six papers in a special issue of the *Marquette Law Review* (Spring 2004), which captures a multidisciplinary perspective on "The Emerging Interdisciplinary Canon of Negotiation."

Docherty has worked with numerous partner organizations to help communities strengthen their capacity to harness the positive energy and minimize the negative consequences of conflict. She is particularly interested in the challenges facing communities and organizations experiencing sudden changes that demand rapid adaptation to new realities, such as a changing population, economic restructuring, changes in laws or regulations, or the losses associated with natural disasters or catastrophic events.

Docherty also works with the Strategies for Trauma Awareness and Resilience (STAR) program, which is a post-September 11 project of Church World Service and Eastern Mennonite University. She earned her doctorate in conflict analysis and resolution at George Mason University.

METHOD OF PAYMENT

❐ Check or Money Order
   *(payable to **Good Books** in U.S. funds)*

❐ Please charge my:
   ❐ MasterCard   ❐ Visa
   ❐ Discover   ❐ American Express

\# _____

exp. date _____

Signature _____

Name _____

Address _____

City _____

State _____

Zip _____

Phone _____

Email _____

SHIP TO: (if different)

Name _____

Address _____

City _____

State _____

Zip _____

Mail order to: **Good Books**
P.O. Box 419 • Intercourse, PA 17534-0419
Call toll-free: 800/762-7171
Fax toll-free: 888/768-3433
Prices subject to change.

Group Discounts for

The Little Book of *Strategic Negotiation* # ORDER FORM

If you would like to order multiple copies of **The Little Book of Strategic Negotiation** by Jayne Seminare Docherty for groups you know or are a part of, use this form. (Discounts apply only for more than one copy.)
Photocopy this page as often as you like.

The following discounts apply:

1 copy	$4.95
2-5 copies	$4.45 each (a 10% discount)
6-10 copies	$4.20 each (a 15% discount)
11-20 copies	$3.96 each (a 20% discount)

To order larger quantities,
please call 800/762-7171 for discounts.
Prices subject to change.

Quantity   *Price*   *Total*

____ copies of **Strategic Negotiation** @ _____ _____

PA residents add 6% sales tax _____

Shipping & Handling
(add 10%; $3.00 minimum) _____

TOTAL _____